Praise For *Cinder Girl Grows Wings*

"You cannot read this collection without holding your breath as author Stephanie Parent guides you through the mysteries, fantasies, and dangers of the underground world of BDSM. Transgressive and profound, *Cinder Girl Grows Wings* is a proclamation and reclamation of femininity, agency, and sexual freedom." –Grace R. Reynolds, Elgin Award Nominated author of *The Lies We Weave*

"Powerful, sensual, and evocative words that women can identify with. Parent's writing weaves together desire, memories, and experiences, which she intricately layers with critiques about the complexities of womanhood, relationships, love, and the unmet expectations of fairytales. Through her raw and unapologetic words, she exposes the weight of society's expectations, and the struggles women and girls face in pursuing perfection. The author's open and honest words dive deep into her sexuality, desires, and experiences in the kink community. *Cinder Girl Grows Wings* unveils the author to be a true confessional poet!" – Rose Ivy, author of *Ink Blot Girl*

"Stephanie Parent's *Cinder Girl Grows Wings* explores the dangers of desire, the inability to know the difference between love and cruelty, and the truth that fairy tales are really horror stories. In this collection Stephanie explores the perils of being a doll, but also the perils that happen when a doll grows flesh and blood and a heart of her own. The desire and yearning are inevitable and relatable yet ultimately her doom. Fire is both friend and foe, it's better for the doll is she does not have desires because desires can draw monsters and pain. This poetry collection is poignant, Stephanie doesn't shy away from describing ugly feelings that I knew all too well as a teenager to feel forbidden and to feel like trash...It is a powerful collection of the power of desire and how hope sometimes is too weak to save us, so we must find other ways to break free of our own bondage. This collection speaks of self-loathing, self-discovery, and breaking illusions. The thought of adopting new eyes and being able to see oneself in a different light, a light that isn't as painful as the first glance. I think my favorite part of *Cinder Girl Grows Wings* is how vulnerable, raw, and honest it is. I love that I can relate to aspects of this collection as a whole while never experiencing the dungeon life firsthand. It is a remarkable, beautiful, wounded thing." –Linda M. Crate, author of *searching stained glass windows for an answer*

Cinder Girl Grows *Wings*

Stephanie Parent

Cinder Girl Grows Wings by Stephanie Parent

© 2025, Stephanie Parent

All rights reserved.

Published in the United States by
Curious Corvid Publishing, LLC, Ohio.

Cover Art by Mitch Green
Formatting and typeface by Ravven White

ISBN: 978-1-959860-57-0

Printed in the United States of America

Curious Corvid Publishing, LLC

PO Box 204

Geneva, OH 44041

This is a work of fiction. Unless otherwise indicated, all the names, characters, businesses, places, events and incidents in this book are either the product of the author's imagination or used in a fictitious manner. Any resemblance to actual persons, living or dead, or actual events is purely coincidental.

www.curiouscorvidpublishing.com

First Edition

Curious Corvid
PUBLISHING

Table of Contents

Kindling

Inferno

Ashes

Phoenix

Kindling

You Learn

You learned, early in life, how to become a doll.

You learned to show emotion in carefully measured doses,
      each tear equal to one pull of the string along your spine.
Just enough to make your owner hold you closer,
      stroke your silky hair, pat that one tear dry.

You learned to be careful. Too much emotion, and your owner
      would wail that you were malfunctioning,
      that your glass eyes might burst.
Your owner would peer at every inch of your porcelain limbs,
      searching for cracks they might need to patch up.
      They would squeeze your rigid wrists, clutching you
      tight, till their worry hurt more than any fear or
      loneliness of your own.

You learned that porcelain is beautiful for its fragility,
      for that moment it seems about to shatter,
      but somehow survives.

You learned how to sit on a shelf and wait and watch.

You learned to yearn for arms around you.

You learned that the wrong arms burned.

You learned that if you held all your thoughts and
      desires inside you, away from your owner's
      prying eyes, your wishes would make their own

kind of heat.
Demanding and furious,
    just like a heart.

You learned to break yourself,
    to crack one porcelain finger,
        then two.

You learned that destruction is the closest thing
    to love.

You learned about masking tape,
    duct tape,
        Super Glue.

You learned that people see what they want to see.
    They see what will keep them from
        breaking.

You learned that life as a doll is no life at all.

You learned that there is so little we choose.

You learned that sometimes, you can't get up and walk.
    Sometimes, there's only one way
        off the shelf.

You learned there's not so much difference

    between a fall

and a jump.

1999

Girls who grew up on Britney and Christina
Our mothers and principals waged wars
Over our bare arms in spaghetti straps
While we snuck peeks at our fathers' *Playboy*s

To be desired and to desire were inseparable for us
The perfume-sample scent of our *Seventeens*
The pages turning like the plot of a fairy tale
Our mermaids' voices for a pair of legs and a prince

To want to be wanted was the female condition
Our shampoo came in bottles half-full of trapped flowers
We were sirens who washed our hair with petals
Our waves tumbled down from towers

We trailed tiny plastic butterflies behind us
A breadcrumb path we'd never follow
We were wonder tale wanderers
From summer forests to strange bedrooms

We made poetry of what we lost
We loved the losing most of all
We owned nothing, we flew and fell—

Is it wrong to say I miss us?

That Darn Cat!

One of my favorite movies as a child, filmed over twenty years before my birth, featured a cat, a sly, devilish creature capable of passing between worlds. The camera followed that darn cat from the plush bedroom of Patti, played by Disney princess Hayley Mills, to the yard of the old nagging neighbor, down twisting Santa Monica alleys and up apartment stairs to the robbers' lair, where the kidnapped bank teller sat strapped to her chair—

That darn cat, beloved by Patti, loathed by the handsome young FBI agent assigned to the case. For only DC—Darn Cat—could lead them to the kidnapped woman. That darn cat, prankster and pest, key to saving a woman's life with one of its nine. We, the viewers, meant to laugh at feline antics, to swoon at Patti and the agent's sweet hints of romance. Meant to root for the bank teller to escape and survive.

And I did—as I watched, I laughed my little girl's laugh. I admired Patti's 1960s outfits and the FBI agent's smooth swagger. I giggled at the untimely intrusion of cat claws.

But something else kept me entranced, watching over and over. Kept me lying on my stomach on the moss green carpet of my childhood living room, head propped in hands, gazing wondrously at the screen:

The quick glimpses, through a feline intruder's eyes, of a gagged woman. Limbs strapped to a chair. Coarse caricatures of robbers manhandling her, threatening her. No escape. I should have been terrified—

So why couldn't my seven, eight, nine-year-old self turn my head? Why couldn't I look away? Why did I want so badly to know how that bound woman might feel?

Why did I suspect that, in the dark places inside of me, the alleys and crawl spaces too tight for humans but right for other, craftier creatures—

That in those secret spaces, I already knew just how she felt?

I had my own gag to wear. The invisible tape tightened, trapping my lips, when I considered asking anyone I knew if they, too, dreamed of restriction and ropes.

My child self knew some things were not for most people to speak or understand. Some places were not for my eyes to see or my feet to tread—

But I envied.

I envied that darn, darn cat, who could go where I could not.

I envied that woman tied to the chair,

who could go nowhere.

Thinner

Here in this house with the ghosts of childhood hopes never
realized, pale nooses slung from burnt-out fairy lights,
I breathe through narrow throat, slide between
tapering halls, wondering—is it better to hold
solid, grow too big for this place and break
through—or is the only escape to become
thinner and thinner, giving up bit by
bit all I once desired and believed I
could own, till I am insubstantial
enough to slip free, weightless
without wishes and dreams,
needing no air in the lace
of my lungs, lightly
slipping through
a crack where
her portrait
once hung
on the
wall?

Read the Stars

I was born on the cusp
between Libra and Scorpio
destined to desire
balance and beauty

                      darkness and danger

the scales

                      the stinger.

Tightroping
imaginary lines
between stars.
Caught in the webs that
connect constellations.

I practiced perfection

                      pushed back prickles of
                      temptation.

Straight A's, college aspirations.
Pointed toes in ballet shoes,
ribs ridged beneath tank tops.
Evaluating equations of
talent and sacrifice:
less of one required
more of the other
to tip the scales in my favor.

                      The older I grew, the more
                      midnight desires intruded,
                      ebony-encased.
                      I wished for a different
                      type of dance, slink and shine
                      beneath spotlights. To become a
                      black hole, absorb men's gazes
                      in my gravity.

I floated, weightless, angelic.

                      I sank, sinful, diabolic.

I divided—
        became binary stars
            fused of
    fire
        and lies
cover jobs
            alibis
"I love yous" spoken through phone lines
            to parents in another galaxy
who only knew the daytime me.
        My orbit swung tighter
scales circling
                arachnids coiling
        limbs twisting round a pole
slipping
              sliding
        fighting the pull of gravity.

    Me, staring at stars, not knowing
            their flames burnt out light-years ago

        I looked heavenward while my
                dreams
degraded
        body swung backwards
            tumbled
            and betrayed me.
I was no ballerina, could not
balance any longer

            I was the scorpion stung
            by its own tail.

The Girl in the Magic Trick

I dreamt of the ropes kissing my wrists
the way some girls dream of Prince Charming's lips
others of white dresses, or white horses
or their bodies on silver screens, voices over radio waves
ascending beyond this world—

My deepest desires were for constriction
thick ropes and silky sashes
alternated the starring roles
confining my limbs, sealing my lips
darkening my vision as my insides
lit up.

I grew older, and feared to speak
my dreams aloud. Whenever I was paired
with another, my desires stayed
silent—my gag, invisible. My limbs
became burdens. In my mind, my body
turned heavy and hideous and cold.

Ashamed, I fled to solitude,
private visions of
railroad tracks—

Till he saw me, snuck up from behind
a silent train derailing me
knocking me flat
bending my body backwards, strapping
me into unnatural

shapes that felt right,
so right that

though I could not move,
I flew.
Blindfolded, I did not foresee
the wreckage; I could not tell
when danger was safety
and when I should have
found scissors

cut through knotted twine, like
knife through gristle

opened my eyes to the
real world

and sawed my own
way out.

Inferno

Capricious Deities

Fire is a trickster god
It lets you hold it in your hands
A flame at the tip of a candle or lighter
A blaze as small as a locket or charm

        But the second you think you know it
        Fire changes its form
        Dragon tongues ravaging a hillside
        Smoke smothering a crowded room

Fire is desire
Ruby embers on a frost-cold
Night

        Fire is disgust
        Scent of burning flesh
        Black like rot

Fire is passion
Consuming oxygen, expanding
Faster than you can blink, filling
Your universe like stars

        Fire is destruction
        Light-years in the making, blasting
        Craters in the ground

Fire is beauty
Burning blue, dancing with

Grace and power no human
Would dare assume

> Fire is monstrosity
> Leaving behind blistered ridges and
> Fissures, offending eyes
> And souls

Fire is divinity
Reanimating what was
Frozen, re-starting
Hearts

> Fire is hell
> Suffering unspeakable
> A fate too terrible
> To be borne

Fire is pure
Elemental, ever-changing
Always renewing
Shifting forms

> But above all

> Fire is devious, dangerous
> And those who choose to
> Dance with it do so at
> Their own risk—yet
> Oh, at least we fly
> Us moths

My Dungeon Love Affair

I fell in love with a dungeon—a dungeon
above ground, a little cottage near the Pacific
Ocean where, behind blacked-out windows, girls in
pink corsets were spanked and flogged
by men who paid well. Where mistresses in black
spanked and flogged men, too. A world I had
never imagined existed, just as I never imagined
I would not always want to wear pink,
would not always want to be spanked,
by any willing hands.

> I fell in love with a boy—a boy who
> loved to spank, maybe more than he ever
> loved me—but I didn't care. With him, at
> night, I reenacted my days at the dungeon,
> brought them to their natural conclusion.
> I begged him, again and again—*hurt me,*
> *violate me, pierce me—*

> hold me.

My two loves began within months
of each other.

> Destined to always remain
> intertwined.

The deep sweet silence of my nights
carried me through the loudest, shrillest days,

the ones where I let out ugly screams
(faked, only sometimes).

The dirtiest deeds of my days
seeped into my pores like seeds
and grew wild, till I carried them
to the bed of the boy I loved.

I wore blindfolds that only slipped off
at the most inopportune of times.

I could no longer tell cruel love from
loving cruelty, weeds from wildflowers;
perhaps I'd never known
the difference at all.

I never imagined love could change so much

What I'd lose

How I'd fall.

A Terrible Idea

Every morning,
my ex took testosterone pills
he ordered off Amazon.
I knew it was a terrible idea but I
could never tell him
what to do.

I knew it was a terrible idea
to fall in love with someone
because of the way he held me
down; the way he slid up behind me after I'd
emerged from the shower, ripped off
the towel and pinned me to
the bed beneath muscles
throbbing, seeds planted potent
beneath his flesh and me,
a crushed pistil. Pollen spilling
across the sheets. Desire the
bloom.

I knew it was a terrible idea
but I was always looking for someone else
to tell me what to do.

I loved him for the way he
held me after, cradled me
in his hands like a wilted
blossom till his touch
resurrected me,

the soft sun
chasing away
the storm.

I wonder, if the hormones
hadn't grown wild through
his veins, bulking his biceps and
boiling his blood, would his
tenderness have lasted long
enough to shelter us when
the sun fled and the
sky froze?

Or would it have been another
terrible idea, to try to weather
out the winter, when all along,
I knew, I should have run?

Confessions of a Professional Submissive

My ass has been spanked
by so many hands—
some thick and calloused
others smooth and tender
masculine and feminine
in ways that don't always
conform to their owner's
gender.

Blindfold me, and I'd like to
say I could identify each touch—
Like to think I would flinch
at a slap from a hand that had
grabbed my pussy, uninvited,
and pinched. Like to think I would
soften at a spanking from a palm
that had rubbed my back, soothed
my fears. Fingers that brushed a stray
hair from my face, dried a tear.

But the truth is:

Despite all I've experienced
in this strange profession of
mine—despite all the kind
and cruel clients, all the
women I've worked beside and
loved in different ways, different
times—

Despite all this, one certainty
I've learned:

A slap is a slap. The impact of
hard hand against malleable skin
will have its desired effect
upon one who was born
to give in.

Rip the blindfold off; I will
keep my eyes closed, gaze down,
head hung. That old song—*hurt-
me-love-me-hurt-me-love-me*—
sounds the same no matter in
what key it's sung.

My Body Has Never Been a Temple

My body has been a spring field sprouting wildflowers birthed to
be ravaged,
blue and blushing blossoms with no names. Viney weeds tangled
with desire,
competing in their clamor to escape the underground, yearning
for the
rough wind and drenching rain.

My body has been a barren field slick with ice, forbidding all
trespassers,
welcoming the snow that conceals cracks and crushed earth
underneath.
Preferring to freeze alone than to melt beneath another's sun.

My body has been a trash heap, the receptacle where I begged
for
sweat and spit and cum, degradation that brought me pride and
pleasure. Made me believe that others saw me and would stay,
would trample me like the earth beneath their boot and pick me
back up again.

Never have I desired to plow soil, plant seeds, pluck blossoms.
I am recipient, supplicant, I lie in wait. A rose is a rose is
a rose. What's sown in fertile earth will always
grow.

Glitter Dust

To your unschooled eyes, the dungeon glimmers
despite its shadows, boundless in its brilliance, so dark
it turns to light. Every lacquered surface polished:
plush carpets, velvet sofas, airbrushed portraits
of women in corsets on the walls.

A wondrous place where your fantasies come to
life in unimagined forms. Six-foot crosses,
walls lined with cuffs and floggers, rainbows
of red and black and purple grown-up toys.

But stay a while, lie face smooshed against
the sticky leather of the spanking bench,
where countless other girls and clients have lain
before you. Breathe in old sweat and desire,
dread and pleasure and acrid fear—

Stay longer, watch men shuffle out in sudden
shame, still zipping their pants, leaving you to
pick up messy towels and messier emotions—

Stay, and see the dust accumulating in the corners.
Clinging to the mirrors. Creeping into the cracks atop
bondage tables and throne chairs.

Linger longer, and the dust starts to
coat your skin. Seeps in till hours
in the shower can't steam it
clear.

Remember how crystal clean
the dungeon first appeared—
how the sparkles shone.
Buy glitter eyeshadow in every shade,
searching out the perfect match
for your green eyes—

The one part of your face not dulled,
flawed, by the dirty dust. Desperately,
try to distract from the disease of
clogged pores, potholed picks,
your own shame come to
monstrous life.

Go home, scrub your skin and apply
fresh layers of face paint, praying for
miracles, a supplicant to the church
of smudged mirrors and cracked hopes.

It never works.

You cannot conceal yourself from him, your
Dom and lover, the one you most want
to appear pure and perfect for.

You cannot conceal, but you must not
let him see your flaws. The bond you
most want to be real and true, now
the one where you're most desperate to
hide.

(You have no choice:
You must run from the things
You desire.)

You are no longer unschooled, you have
learned:

Fantasies draw danger, like metal to
magnets. Shadows are not reliable
cloaks. Glitter fades, and your
ugliness always seeps to the surface,
so much stronger than
beauty or
hope.

Frequently Asked Questions at the Dungeon

1. Are you allowed to take off your underwear?
2. Do you *really* like getting spanked?
3. What's that toy with the long handle over there called? Can I use it?
4. Are you sure you can't take off your underwear?
5. Do you do nipple torture? Does that mean I can bite your nipples?
6. Do you do this at home? Do you have a boyfriend? A girlfriend, then?
7. Why can't you take off your underwear?
8. Does that hurt?
9. Does *that* hurt?
10. Does that feel good?
11. Do you want to touch my cock?
12. Couldn't you take off your underwear, just for me? Just this one time?
13. Does that *really* tickle? I bet it would tickle more if you let me get closer to your—
14. Do you like working here?
15. What if you just moved your underwear to the side, like this—
16. We could make this so much more fun, couldn't we?

17. Why can't I see your pussy? I told you I'd let you touch my cock.

18. Okay, well, maybe next time? I'll be back next week.

Sometimes, at the Dungeon

I became a doll.
My limbs rigid, yet pliable all at once.
I stood still, eyes down, as strangers' hands
arranged me into shapes
domestic and
erotic.

I pictured myself in their homes
naked in a kitchen, a dining room
forever frozen stirring a spoon in a saucepan
balancing a dish over a table
or in the bedroom, bent over
ass up.

Maybe a tiny piece of me
went home with each client
became a statue haunting their hallways
invisible to wives and children
though they shivered, sensing the ghosts
of husbands' and fathers' secrets
every time they passed me by.

Doll-me, the villain of someone else's
story, even if that someone never knew me,
or suspected why her love lingered
away from home.

Doll-me, the object of lonely men's
desire, decorating every corner of their

empty homes and minds.
Real-me, learning so well
how to be still and silent.

I feared and hoped to be trapped
forever, perfect as plastic,
ecstatically existing
through someone else's
eyes.

He Called Me Doll

He called me doll
like he was a mobster in a 1950s movie
like Frank Sinatra or Marlon Brando
like I was his perfect plastic plaything
who could never do anything wrong.

He called me doll
and every time he pulled the string on my back
I performed a new trick
like Tiny Tears and Dancerina,
Betsy Wetsy and Little Miss Echo,
speaking only in the voice of
her owner.

He called me doll
tucked me in his coat like Polly Pocket
took me along to watch while he
flirted with other girls.
Sometimes he invited them home
so they could play with me too.

He called me doll
and I was so overjoyed to be the one
he kept in his toybox
that my heart began to transform,
plastic melting into flesh and blood,
beating new emotions into veins
that now flowed.

He called me doll
but he did not like my new tricks:
the human muscles and joints I grew.
The ones I used to embrace, but also
to push or pull or twist away.
The words I spoke that weren't echoes,
that could be more scream
than song.

He called me doll
and I did not want to lose him.
I could not imagine
never again being his doll.
I could not conceive of the hollow
that would carve itself around
my now human heart.

He called me doll
even when he was angry.
Even when he wondered
why we couldn't just go back
to the way things were before.
Even when he demanded to know
why I couldn't remain posable as
plastic.

He called me doll
and I performed one more trick:
I got up on wobbly flesh-and-blood legs,
and I left.

Only Cursed Desires

I lost all my kinks in a battle with a
monster much stronger than
I. They fell one by one:

Spitting was the first I surrendered
when blemishes bloomed across
my face
where I had welcomed
another human's bacteria
where I'd desired to be dirty and degraded
but only if I could wash the muck off…
decontaminate myself.

Along with the blemishes
came layers of heavy foundation,
frantic attempts to hide my
shame
       (because it wasn't the sexy
       kind any longer)
and then the gags and blindfolds
had to go—the way they left
peeling patches in the makeup mask
I'd spent hours applying
the artificial-orange stains creeping across
the insides of the blindfolds, the
straps of the gags
proclaiming that I was no longer a
perfectly natural, naturally
perfect girl.

Soon I felt so dirty
in all the wrong ways.
I suspected I did not deserve
to be played with at all—I was a doll
destined for the rubbish heap—
and so, to justify my beliefs,
I obsessively looked for more flaws:

Bumps on my arms
clogged pores covering
my chest and back
butt blemishes
ingrown hairs.

They rose up like monsters, like
Medusa's snakes from her scalp.

My raging, restless mind
sent impulses all the way down
to my fingernails, those compulsive critters—

I picked myself raw.

And that was when
my kinks started dropping
like disordered flies.

I couldn't be tied up, because then
how would I contort myself, a
desperate circus freak, ensuring
my hair fell just so
to hide my greatest defects?

I couldn't be flogged on my
marred shoulders.
I couldn't be spanked on my
red-skinned, ruined
rear end.

I couldn't, couldn't, couldn't
do anything but destroy
the body I'd longed so badly
to give away
to offer up—

My mind twisted desire
into decay
the final, all-consuming kink
$$(O - C - D)$$
of a broken brain.

Duct

Duct tape is for fixing,
patching tears, hiding holes.
You can keep air from escaping an
inner tube, water from leaking out
a hose—

Make things work
a little

longer.

Draw out
the expiration

date.

He put duct tape over my lips,
play-acting one of those old detective
movies we both loved. He was the villain
capturing me, the damsel in distress,
pinning my hands above my head.
His mouth touched storm-shaded
polyethylene, and on the other side,
mine.

I could not taste the bitterness behind
his tongue, the way I had the previous day,
a new aversion I could not hide. With the
tape to keep me safe, I did not

turn away.

The pressure of his lips felt like
love from a distance. I remembered a time
when we did not need patching up, when
I needed no binds beyond my mind,
my heart.

Breathing plastic and rubber, smelling sweat
and cologne, I found peace. I let myself forget
what happens when you leave duct tape
on too long.

His hands/
        my lips

the rip/
        the rupture

the burn

      of a betrayal

      the betrayal

of a burn.

Rejects

I could not stand myself
could not sit with myself either
or sleep with myself, or gaze
at myself in a mirror, so I
rejected them along with
myself.

With hair falling over my pimpled cheek,
hand floating above my pockmarked chin,
in the interview room at the dungeon I said:

Our session's not working for me anymore
It just doesn't feel like a good fit
It's not you, it's me

As if this were some casual romance
A final meeting in a coffee shop

> In my old life, before I changed
> my name, wore fancy lingerie
> the only thing worse than being
> rejected
> was to reject
> someone else
>
> Every time I contemplated another's
> loneliness, another's pain
> a sick, soiled feeling would rise up
> inside me: my stomach about to overturn

its contents, mouth tasting of tripwires,
lungs unable to take in air

Now, with all my own sickness, my
ugliness seeping up and up and up,
root rot, I had no room left to care
about someone else

I shielded myself the only way
I could:
          My protection, their rejection
Thorns inside my armor
hiding me, yet
lacerating me
still

(And it wasn't till years later, when I'd rejected them all—even
the one I loved, the one whose bed I shared and lips I kissed, the
one whose touch was petals and pinpricks, whose presence was
the peaks and plummets of a drug I could not give up—only
years later, did I truly consider how those men must have felt)

The men I abandoned
could never have envisioned
the monster I imagined myself to be
the sensation of dirt crawling into every
crevice of my skin, seeping through
the corners of my closed lips and
coating my tongue, sliding down
my esophagus to fill up every
piece of me—

All they saw was a girl,
maybe not perfect but pretty enough,
who did not want them, even if
they paid

So I play-acted a thousand breakups, and
all along I clung to the one man who'd shared
my bed, my nights, hoping he would wait
for me, till I found a way to
cleanse myself, to
bloom again

I clutched his limbs, skin, clothes, but
closed my eyes to him because I could
not bear to see myself—

When I opened my eyes, he'd been
gone, they'd all been gone, for
so long—nothing left but
barren ground.

All Fairy Tales Are Horror Stories

The fairy tale heroines chopped off their
hands to save their fathers, their fingers to
save their brothers, their tower-long hair to save
themselves. Compared to such extremes, what
I did was not insanity, not even worthy of
mention, not much at all:

I simply excavated my imperfections, gouged
them right out of my skin. Goodbye to every
bump and blemish; hello to pits and pockmarks,
swollen surfaces I could do nothing to calm,
horror I was helpless to stop.

I was trapped in the Bluebeard's castle of my
body—I had used the wrong key, peered into the
wrong room. Discovered stains I could not
scrub off.

I began to believe the only solution would be
to gouge out my eyes, stop seeing the flaws. Throw
myself from the tower in which I'd locked myself, land
on a bed of thorns, impale body and soul.

I had imagined myself Rapunzel, but instead I
became her prince—the one who had not saved
her from the witch. The one who lost his sight and
roamed desolate lands, searching for his lover or
for himself.

How many tears would it take to clear my vision?
How long could I squeeze salt water from a stone?
If I walked forever, could I be rescued, could I
rescue myself, could I leave behind

the body I'd

broken?

Wildfire

the city where i found my dungeon, my lovers and torturers, was known for its conflagrations. we humans who lived there did our best to cause destruction: our tiny earthquakes and infernos, the ways we struck each other's flesh, arrowed cruel words into minds and planted them deep in beating hearts. but the earth watched our little battles, our victories and defeats—the pain growing inside us till we believed it so big, it could smother an entire world. the earth watched, and it laughed, harder and harder till it quaked and we measured its seismic waves. harder still, till the earth could not keep from opening its mouth. every year, it consumed us with fiery tongues, reminding us our little pains were pinpricks. we, with our dreams and desires and suffering, were the playthings of the universe, all discardable dolls. our struggles were ash riding the santa anas,

dust raining down the mountains,

debris lost to the endless saltwater blue.

Ashes

Ugly Love

I wanted to be lovely so I made myself ugly

Flint and tinder lived close together in my mind

Always in danger of colliding, igniting strange

Obsessions, kindling wild, nonsensical, blazing binds

Wishing to be worthy of love, never daring to believe it

I aimed for perfection, plummeted like a shooting

Star. Scarred as I collided with cold, unforgiving earth

Instead of standing, brushing off the dirt

I rolled around in the muck, let it penetrate

Every scrape and scratch and seep deep inside so

I would know I was infected, know I was not

Deserving of love, so I would have an excuse to dig

Deeper into the debris where I'd fallen

And bury myself
Never again, I promised my hopes, my heart

Never risk igniting

flaming

desiring

yearning

Never glow

Never burn

To glory

Or to ash

Sacrifice

Desire was my religion.

My want for them to want me
overtook my sky, great clouds
descending from the heavens.
My body's own needs,
flowers withering without
sun, meant less than

nothing.

I was a worshipper
yearning to be made into an idol.

Placed on a pedestal,
trapped under glass—
a blossom in a greenhouse.

I did not understand
the consequences of desire,
how idols are created to be
    broken down

    receptacles
for another's excrement.

Abandoned
to bleed out.

My belly filled with
my own regrets, clawing from the
inside out.

I had made the wrong choice
not to own what was mine
to hollow it out, give it away
strap myself to the cross and await
attention and abandonment both.

As if anyone else's

eyes/hands

desire/degradation

devotion/desertion

anyone else's religion
could ever define

who I am

what I own.

The Longest Goodbye

Farewell to stinging touches and soft ones, sweeter
for the cruelty that had come before. I was never a drinker,
but I could have used some liquid courage to face the world,
again, on my own. Instead I licked dry, lonely lips
and wrapped my bare skin in a coat. As if its fabric was
your hands, harsh and soothing and no longer
mine to know.

Farewell to a life like a streetlamp lighting the way
through city rain, a guide wavering but true.
Farewell to you leading me forward, my
imagination clothing you in a
Bogart trench coat

—gone. My life insurance lost. Just me, abandoned in
that noir city, maze of alleys and fire escapes and
window blinds, no color left, only black and white.
Your fedora in my hands, the one I stole; but though
it would have shielded my face from the downpour,
I could not put it on.

Farewell to three-way rendezvous in other cities,
open car windows on the 101, hotel sheets and
misty ocean mornings. After you shared me, you
held me like we were the only two survivors in an
apocalyptic world. Maybe I should have saved
my money, learned to drive, vacationed up the
coast and bought a country home. Instead
I nuzzled heartache in my mouth like the

barrel of a gun.
If only we had broken things off in person, perhaps
I could have said a shorter goodbye. Could have put on my
coat and hat, gathered my weapons, my unspoken
words. I could have been the one to take the last walk
out of the room. But the two of us were never so
simple, so easily defined.

So here is my poem, my bullet, my last
farewell: in my memory you will always
be lovely, I will always be saying
goodbye.

Phoenix

Born This Way

Tell me I'm beautiful
> and I'll show you my ugly

I was born with eyes
> that see the mud before the wildflowers

The pollution before the stars

> I was born imagining myself

in a cage of my own creation
> tried to blame childhood tragedy

parents with poor coping mechanisms
> boundaries blasted open, baby skin

slippery with greedy, needy touch

But—
> my heart beat inside a ribcage

that resembled bars
> I knew my makeup, no nurture taught

me
what nature had made me
> inevitable, ingrained like wood

inevitable that once I got what I
> wanted, I would have to destroy it

> do as I ask

make my cage real and solid, and
> I'll beat myself bloody on spiked bars

give me a porcelain doll
                    I'll tear the silk hair from her scalp
crack her flesh, gouge out her
                    eyes

destroy the surface, till I must
                    find a new way to hide the
hideous insides, burrow and bury myself
                    like a seed till all I have is
a messy, murderous, miraculous
                    multitude of words

just small enough
                    just powerful enough
to slide out from between
                    bars.

Nine Lives, Two Eyes

Cats have nine lives, they say
and us humans aren't as lucky
but I hope we get at least two.

After I grew up, tried on a few
half-lives and assumed identities
of my own, I watched *That Darn Cat* again.
I saw the actors differently
this time around.

I saw that the bank teller gagged and strapped to a chair
was not the lovely young woman I remembered—
she was older, face tight and tired; her dyed-orange hair
glaring, her expression severe. I had mixed her up
with other fantasies, other damsels in distress,
over the passing of so many years.

I saw that Hayley Mills, the leading lady
I'd always imagined to be so perfect, had acne
beneath her 1960s pancake makeup.
My own skin crawled to witness it.
The memories of bumps and clogs were phantoms
I could not exorcise, scars I could not
conceal.

I found, to my greater surprise, that
Hayley was beautiful still.

Maybe I couldn't earn new lives—

but could I adopt new eyes?
I could not escape my flesh,
but could I transform it through
perspective alone, a painter
re-evaluating a
tableau?

Could I wipe away tears and glass shards,
clear my vision, wait out a dark forest night
till dawn?

Would branches turn back from
grasping witch's claws, reveal their true
nature as harmless wood?

Would leaves and petals unfurl in the
morning's fresh sunlight,
buds open—

Each stamen and pistil
a tiny new life.

Each still on the TV screen
a familiar surprise.

The Woolsey Witches

witch trees burned black by the fires
that raged through malibu last year

witch trees stripped of their leaves and defenses
turned by some dark alchemy
starker and stronger
altered beautiful

ten months ago, the witch trees were green
consumed
by sorcerous flame
as i sat outside a coffee shop
breathing ash
typing my life away, racing deadlines
running to respectable tutoring jobs
and less respectable meetings with men
grasping for paper bills to feed the fire-monsters of
greedy los angeles that takes,
takes till you can't get ahead, can't keep up, can't
breathe
while beyond me, in the
distance
malibu burned

ten months after the fires, on a rare day
not full of work (which steals more soul: teaching
kids to get good grades like little machines, staring at
caustic computer screens, giving more pieces of my
lost cause body away?)

i walk along a creek in malibu
and see witch trees
black and bare and beautiful
casting their spells
against twilight colors of purpling brush,
splashs of electric where the sun hits
new green
fairy-tale forest
forged from the smoke

and i remember—the name unearthed,
a surprise, from beneath the years since
i've stopped reading for pleasure
or hope—
vixanne wigg, witch baby's black magic mother
in the fairy-tale novels of los angeles i
devoured, as a young, greedy girl,
as though i were fire
consuming the pages and the dreams
upon them
alchemizing them, absorbing them
making them part of my bones
so that someday i would have to
journey to that fairy-tale city
myself

and now, as i touch a witch
tree, pockmarked bark like keloid
growths, ugly up close, my anger
ignites, at the author of those books
for selling a dream that's real and
not real

dangling but just out of
reach
and at the foolish girl who bought that
dream
not understanding the price

the witch trees are beautiful
from farther away
limbs the deep black
of something that has suffered
and survived
and i wish i could find that beauty
in a body that gave too much away
wish i could find that beauty
in the way
i threw myself to the flames
allowed them to kiss and lick and
linger
till my skin
rebelled
bubbled and blistered as if burnt
and i saw myself a witch, a monster
picked and clawed at myself so
i'm scarred
like the witch trees

but i can't see beauty
yet (will i ever
see?)
so i keep working, giving
pieces of myself to the
machines and to the

men, hoping
if i can buy the right potion
one day i'll douse the flames,
brush off the ash and transmute to something
pure

eyes on my computer
screen
on my flesh that must be
fixed
while beauty dangles around me
casting its spell
beyond my reach

but on this day, in malibu,
i am not teaching children
or meeting men
i am climbing a hill in the summer
heat, beneath witch trees that give no
shade
until i reach
a waterfall
a wispy thing, a trickle of
liquid, a hint of a
breeze

not enough to put out a
fire
but maybe enough—for
now—to
breathe.

Little Wings

I scrawled my love on a piece of paper
and grew angry when a flame devoured it
and left ash

I typed my hopes on a computer keyboard
and panicked when a virus darted and danced in lines of code
like a trickster god across the screen

I carved my dreams in a great old oak tree
and when the thunder bellowed and the lightning
cleaved my dreams in two, my heart went with them

So I wrote my secrets on my skin
but when the cells divided, peeled and shed
my secrets with them,

I grew despondent,
spoke my losses to the wind,
thought it would carry them far from me

But instead
it stirred the ash
and made the electric lines sing
like ancient deities
and scattered the seeds across the soil
and raised the hairs up on my arms
like little wings

Cinder Girl Grows Wings

Maybe fairy tales were my first kink.
The ultimate tease and denial:

Sleep in ashes and sweep enough floors
and you, too, will win princes and wealth.
So said Disney and the Brothers Grimm, in
their different palettes. Technicolor or
chiaroscuro, I devoured them
indiscriminately. My fetishes
whittled down to the finest
intricacies:

The jagged pink spikes of Cinderella's
dress, after her sisters got their hands
on it, on her. Her hopes more beautiful
for being torn.

The glowing tip of a spindle, perilous
and lovely. Sharp enough to penetrate
my flesh and, deeper still, my
dreams.

The precise details of a story—
three drops of blood spilled
from an ebony window onto white
snow. Not two, not four—
Exactly. Three.

Fairy tales offered the steps of a spell: a

story of sacrifice and pain, a vow of
witness and rescue, a Dom cradling
their cane-striped, shaking sub after
a scene. The fantasy promising fulfillment
that never quite lasted, always danced,
a shimmering enchantment, just beyond
my reach.

Until I found myself older, awakening
alone in ashes, disillusioned, throat
coated with soot and eyes tearing
against the sting.

Only so long could I
suffer for a dream.

I turned to a different genre of stories,
a different kind of kink. Tales of
winged creatures rising from ashes,
a fetish for transformation, a firebird
burning my love for my own pain
away.

No more waiting among the cinders
for someone to listen, to save me, to see.
Just me, doll turned girl, sending my stories
of strange desires
                out into the universe—
                                another sort of

exhibitionism,

                        soaring on fiery

            wings.

Acknowledgments

Several of these poems appeared in altered form online or in print, including "You Learn" in *Burningword Literary Journal,* "1999" in *The Daily Drunk,* "Read the Stars" in *Suburban Witchcraft,* "The Girl in the Magic Trick" in *My Say in the Matter,* "My Body Has Never Been a Temple" in *Outcast Press,* "A Terrible Idea" in *Olney Magazine,* "Thinner" in *Pink Plastic Press,* "Confessions of a Professional Submissive" in *Moist Poetry,* "Duct" in *Querencia Press Fall Anthology,* "Sacrifice" in *The Dark Side of Purity Zine,* "The Woolsey Witches" in *Corvid Queen,* "Little Wings" in *Royal Rose Magazine,* and "Cinder Girl Grows Wings" in *Querencia Press Summer Anthology.*

"You Learn," "1999," "Read the Stars," "My Body Has Never Been a Temple," "A Terrible Idea," "Confessions of a Professional Submissive," "Only Cursed Desires," and "Cinder Girl Grows Wings" also appeared in the microchapbook *Doll Ashes, Cinder Wings* from Maverick Duck Press.

About The Author

Stephanie Parent is a graduate of the Master of Professional Writing program at the University of Southern California as well as a professional submissive and switch.

After working for six years at a commercial dungeon in Los Angeles, she's now writing about her personal and professional experiences with BDSM for publications including the HuffPost, Hippocampus, Pithead Chapel, Entropy, The Whorticulturalist and Mookychick. Her work has been anthologized in Dating & Sex: The Mutual Theory of Self-Destruction and Slut Vomit: An Anthology of Sex Work.

Stephanie is also a published author of poetry and fiction; her poetry has been nominated for the Rhysling Award and Best of the Net, and her flash fiction won the O:JA&L Editor's Prize for Flash Discourse.

Her first poetry collection, Every Poem a Potion, Every Song a Spell, was released August 2022 from Querencia Press. Her debut gothic horror novel, The Briars, is forthcoming in May 2023 from Cemetery Gates Media.

Born and raised in Baltimore, Maryland, Stephanie now considers Los Angeles her true home.